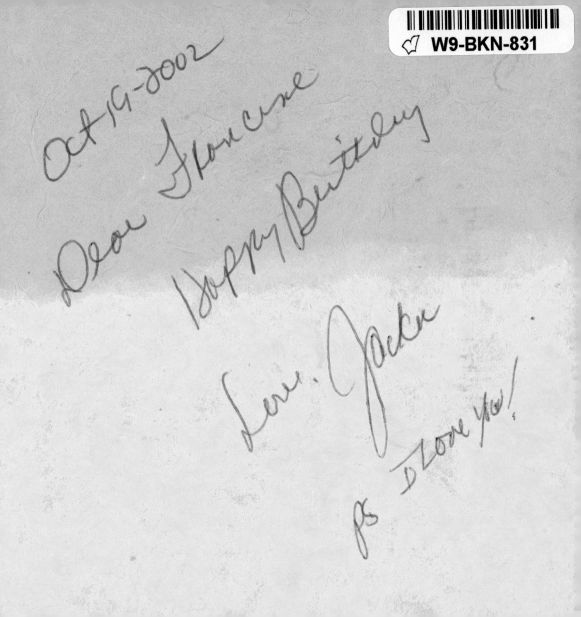

Oct 19-2002

Dear Francine

Happy Birthday

Love, Jack

PS "I Love you!"

*Sister, if I could give you the happiness
and success that you deserve,
it would last forever.
I wish you all that you desire
and all that is beautiful.
You will forever be a part
of me and my life,
because you have a place in my heart.*

~ Victor Barbella

Sister,
You Have a Special Place in My Heart

...What It Means to Share a
Lifetime of Memories,
Friendship, and
Love

SPS Studios ™

Boulder, Colorado

Library of Congress Catalog Card Number: 2001005445
ISBN: 0-88396-613-1

ACKNOWLEDGMENTS appear on page 48.

Certain trademarks are used under license.

Manufactured in Thailand
First Printing: January 2002

 This book is printed on recycled paper.

Library of Congress Cataloging-in-Publication Data

Sister, you have a special place in my heart : — what it means to share a lifetime of memories, friendship, and love.
    p. cm.
ISBN 0-88396-613-1 (hardcover : alk. paper)
1. Sisters — Quotations, maxims, etc. I. SPS Studios.
PN6084.S56 S558 2001
306.875 — dc21

2001005445
CIP

SPS Studios, Inc.
P.O. Box 4549, Boulder, Colorado 80306

Contents

(Authors listed in order of first appearance)

Sister, You Have a Special Place in My Heart

There is never a time in my life
when I'm not with you in some way.
There are moments when you
come to mind more strongly,
sometimes in a special way,
but you are with me always.
Sometimes you are with me
in the warm memory
of some laughter we've shared.
I admire your personality,
your character, and
the qualities you possess.
You are a capable
and determined person.

There is an understanding
we have developed,
a relationship that shows we care,
and a oneness that has grown
out of respect, patience, and love.
If I could give you the happiness
and success that you deserve,
it would last forever.
I wish you all that you desire
and all that is beautiful.
You will forever be a part
of me and my life,
because you have a place in my heart.

~ Victor Barbella

I Am Honored to Call You My Sister and Fortunate to Call You My Friend

I know that I can trust you
with my most cherished treasures,
with my heart and soul, and
with every secret I hold.
I know that you will listen
without criticizing me for my mistakes.
You hear what I am trying to say,
even when I fail to express myself clearly.
I know that I can believe you
without worrying that you will mislead me,
because you are honest with me
even when honesty means disagreement.

I know that you will accept me,
despite every wrong turn I've taken
and every bad decision I've made.
You simply love who I am.
I know that our hearts are connected
on the deepest level.
You know me so well;
your insight and your view of me
make me feel complete.
I know that I am special
because you are so special.
I'm proud of our friendship and
the strength we have together.
I am honored to call you my sister
and fortunate to call you my friend.

~ Regina Hill

Sister, You Are
a Gift to Me

Having you for a sister is one of life's
   priceless gifts.
As children, we shared our triumphs
and depended on each other for support.
We loved each other beyond words.
We shared a bond of love, trust,
   and friendship;
we had a history of memories.
As long as we had each other,
our dreams were never out of reach.
We shared smiles and dreams,
laughter and tears.
We had a love that brought us comfort
and aspirations that gave us hope
   for our future.

Even though we've gotten older,
I am forever grateful for the love we share.
As time passes, I realize how much
   you are a part of me.
Our lives have changed a lot
   since we were young,
but one thing that will never change
is how very much you mean to me.
Thank you for bringing so much joy
   to my life.
You are so precious to me,
and I love you very much.

~ Shannon M. Lester

You Are the Most Beautiful Person I Know...

Not just outside, but inside, too.
You have a wonderful sense of humor,
a loyalty that not many people have,
and a gift of love you give to others.
We may not be perfect ~
we have our share of arguments and troubles.
Yet we can always trust
each other with anything.
When you just have to share something,
good or bad, I will listen.
You are the world to me.
Words can't express my appreciation,
but it means a lot to me that you are my sister,
and I will love you forever.
A sister like you
is the greatest gift in the world.

~ Kristy Jorgensen

I Wish You Life's Best

I wish that the sun will always shine for you, and that your world will always be bright and warm and beautiful.

I wish the wonder of life's sweetest moments for you, with hours full of happiness and days when everything goes the best it can. I wish a million great beginnings for you, with a perfect parade of all your dreams come true and happy endings always.

I wish with all my heart for your greatest happiness. I wish you nothing but the brilliant and vibrant colors of the rainbow and life's brightest days... because the sun should always shine for you.

~ Barbara J. Hall

There's No One like a Sister

A sister is a part of your life
that you can never separate from.
Whether she's older or younger,
through all your formative years,
she shared your pain and sorrow,
your happiness and joy ~
even when you were not aware
that she was there.
A sister protects you from all harm
and is always near when you need her.
She's a friend who listens forever
when others turn away.
She has the broadest shoulders
for you to lean on,
and never complains that you
cause too much trouble.

She asks for little in return ~
just a portion of your time,
a few precious moments
to exchange secrets as only sisters can do.
She brings sunshine where there are clouds;
she is like a breath of spring
through the storms of winter,
a guiding star in the darkness of night.
She smiles at you when others frown
and she welcomes you with open arms.
She accepts you for who you are
and doesn't expect you to be anyone else.
She thinks that you're the best,
and makes you feel so important
that you start to believe it yourself.
There's no one like a sister...
and there's no sister like you!

~ Geri Danks

No matter what life holds for you,
you'll always have me...

No one ever really knows
what life has in store,
what roads they will travel,
or how things will turn out.
It's kind of scary sometimes,
looking ahead and not knowing,
but I want you to know
that you'll always have me.
It doesn't matter where I am
or what I'm doing;
I will always take time for you.
You are a very special person to me,
and you have a place in my heart
that will always be there for you.
I want you to remember
that you will never really be alone,
because you'll always have me
to care about you.

~ Beth Fagan Quinn

To the Angel in My Life...
My Sister

Sometimes you are lucky enough
to experience (and recognize)
a glimpse of the light that is
Knowledge and Love
in the purest of forms,
and an unseen hand pauses
to touch your brow
and smooth away uncertainty and fear.
Some of us call this hand an angel...

When an angel touches you,
you are left with a feeling of peace,
a message of hope, and a brighter life.

I want to thank you
for being one of the angels
who has alighted upon my spirit
and blessed my life.

~ Gina Breitkreutz

The Nine Secrets
of Our Sisterhood

1. We stay close. No matter how busy we are, we make time for keeping in touch. As sisters, we're never more than a heartbeat apart.

2. We spread happiness. When we have news to tell, we focus on the upbeat. We share jokes and laughter. In sad times, we fill one another with hope.

3. Our bond is one of respect. We value our differences, share our talents, and nurture one another's potential.

4. When it comes to each other's activities, we express interest. We are passionately interested in each other's life. That's what more~than~close friends are for.

5. We give each other support. We are the shelter in each other's storms. We lift each other's spirits and cheer one another on.

6. We are tops when it comes to trust. I can trust you with my secrets, and you can truly believe that I will keep yours under lock and key. We are loyal in sisterly love and devoted in our friendship.

7. We treasure our family memories. We are proud of where we came from, and we honor those who are our real~life family heroes.

8. We give each other personal attention. We listen with our hearts and help each other meet needs. We share the promise that someone will always be there to care about us.

9. We promote each other's success. We put any envy aside to promote one another. We are each other's highest achievement seekers.

These are the nine secrets of our sisterhood ~ but it's <u>no</u> secret that our sisterhood is at the top of our list of things to be thankful for.

~ Jacqueline Schiff

Girls will be girls
and friends will be friends,
but when you think of
sisters being sisters,
you know exactly how close
the feelings can be.
Sisters have a special way
of growing closer as the years go by,
and the feelings they have shared
are always a very important part
of their lives.

And though sisters may disagree at times,
they ultimately accept each other
for the way they are,
and they know that
what really matters is the love
they feel for one another.

~ Deanna Beisser

You Have Done So Much for Me

You took my hand
and led me across every broken bridge
over each unconquerable mountain
and through fearful escapades
You took my heart and felt for me
when I couldn't feel any longer
quieting my fears
You warmed my heart
when it was too cold to press on
You brought me smiles
and flowers for my soul
cheering me up when life brought me down
You are my sister and you are
the greatest person in my life
And after all life has dealt us
after all we've been through
I know more than anything
that you are my best friend

~ Vincent Arcoleo

You're My Definition
of a Great Sister!

A great sister is someone
who knows how to share
her clothes and her books with me
and who allows me to join in
with her friends
and have fun together.

A great sister is someone
who is willing to talk late at night
about feelings,
and then not gossip about them
with everyone the next day.
She understands what it means
to need someone
who is sincere and trustworthy.

This is what being a great sister
is all about.
In case you didn't know it,
I think you're one of the best sisters
anyone could ever have.
You do so many nice things for me,
and you care about my happiness.

So today, even though
a thousand other things
are happening in our lives,
I wanted to let you know
that I think you're a great sister.
I'm really glad for
the close relationship that we have.

~ Dena DiJaconi

Growing Up with You Gave Me a Lifetime of Great Memories

From the time I can remember,
I loved you and couldn't stand you
   all at the same time.
I remember silly secrets
   that made us laugh until we couldn't breathe,
stupid fights that made us cry,
and hurtful words thrown out in anger
   yet forgotten minutes later.

We have taken different paths in our lives,
but they've always run side by side,
crossing often and keeping in touch.
We share more than parents and our childhood;
no one else in the world
understands me the way that you do.
We have something special: each other.

~ Cynthia Gruner

When Sisters Become Friends...

As family, sisters share
   a very secure closeness.
But when friendship emerges
   from their closeness,
something even more special happens...
A strong bond develops that brings them
even closer to each other.
The bond is so powerful that
   it not only brings them added joy;
it also comforts and befriends each sister with
loyalty, compassion, and understanding beyond measure.
Regardless of differences, miles between them,
or anything else that can separate them,
sisters who become friends are
always a part of each other.
They are the answer to each other's
   spoken and unspoken needs
and always a gift of love
   to each other's heart.

~ Susan Hickman Sater

A Sister's Love
Is Something to Cherish

A sister's love
is a love that fills the heart
with the sounds of laughter
echoing through time ~
a sentimental soul to share your journey
and all the dreams between
the dark and the bright.
A sister's heart
is a place of warmth and caring,
written on the pages of your life ~
a hand to lift your chin up
when you're down,
someone to hold on to
who is moved with sympathy.

A sister's power
is sunlight for your shadows
and memories growing stronger
through the winds of yesterday ~
the eyes that see within your very being
all the good things you are yet to be.
A sister is a thousand memories
ringing their bells across your destiny ~
all the happy sounds
of grace, love, and laughter.
A sister is someone
you'll always be so very grateful for.

~ Linda E. Knight

No One Knows Me Better than You

*O*ur hearts are intertwined in a
history of shared memories.
We lived the same childhood,
broke many of the same rules,
and learned lessons from each
other and from life.
Because of this, you understand not
only where I've come from, but
who I really am.
We each have chosen our own path
in life. Yet our paths inevitably
converge again and again as time
goes by, for we never lose sight
of their origin.

Over the years, we've talked and laughed,
   listened and cried, supported and
   understood in ways no one else could.
   Even when we don't see eye to eye, I
   know you only want the best for me ~
   just as I do for you.
No matter what else happens in my life ~
   no matter how many times I change
   direction or make mistakes ~ I know
   you will always be there for me.
Your love is very special. It centers me
   and takes me back. It challenges me
   and leads me forward. I'm so glad that
   we will always be sisters and friends.

~ Pamela Koehlinger

Sister, I Hope You Remember All the Things That Dreams Are Made Of

Remember: if you can dream it, you can probably make it come true. Build wonderful bridges to get where you're going. Appreciate all the special qualities within you.

Don't let worries get in the way of recognizing how great things can be. Don't look back; always move ahead. Live to the fullest; make each day count. Don't let the important things go unsaid.

Don't just have minutes in the day; have moments in time. Balance out any bad with the good you can provide. Know that you are capable of amazing results. Surprise yourself by discovering new strength inside.

Add a meaningful page to the diary of each day.
Do things no one else would even <u>dream</u> of. There
is no greater gift than the kind of inner beauty
you possess. Do the things you do... with love.

Walk along the pathways that enrich your happiness.
Taking care of the "little things" is a big necessity.
Don't be afraid of testing your courage. Life is short,
but it's long enough to have excitement <u>and</u> serenity.

Do the things that brighten your life and help you on
your way. Don't just dream of a successful journey;
<u>begin</u> <u>it</u>. Know how much I care about you.

And remember...
    one of life's nicest presents
        is your presence in it.

~ Collin McCarty

You Light Up the World

On the day you came into this world,
a beautiful star dropped from the sky
and landed in your heart.
You carry this wondrous light
within your soul,
and as you grow older
it begins to shine brighter,
making the world a happier place.
I think you are amazing,
truly unique in your kindness
and loving heart.
You touch the hearts of those around you,
sharing the incredible gift of you
and making me so proud to be your sister.
I only hope that one day
I can shine as brightly as you do.

~ Deana Marino

Never Forget This, My Sister...

The sun keeps shining
even when the clouds roll in.
Though they may block the view
for a short time,
together we can chase them away
and find happy days again.
I know things aren't always easy,
but I want you to remember that
I'll be behind you every step of the way,
reminding you how wonderful you are
and how bright the days ahead will be.
Just know that life does not give us
more than we can handle.
But when it seems that way,
I'll be right beside you ~ ready to
ease your heart and lighten your load.
Together we will clear the skies
to brighter days.

~ Vincent Arcoleo

I Love All the Times
I Share with You

In our busy lives, we seldom get the time together that we'd like to have ~ to relax and confide in one another or to enjoy a few moments of quiet reflection. Usually it's rushing and interruptions, quick calls and short visits. Sometimes I think that if we didn't purposely set aside some time to get together, we'd never see each other!

But that's the beauty of our relationship ~ we always manage to make time to be together. And no matter the time or distance that separates us, the bond we share is constant and sure.

I know that I can depend on you in any emergency or for any favor. I know you understand my moods, my needs, my heart. I can always count on you to laugh with me (that is one of my favorite things about us), and I probably laugh with you more than with anyone else in the world.

I can always count on you to listen and to be honest when you disagree, yet I'm secure in the knowledge that no disagreement or problem will ever be big enough to come between us.

You are one of the most important people in my life. There are sisters and there are friends, but it doesn't get any better than having the love and memories I share with my sister combined with the humor, respect, and fun we share as friends.

~ Barbara Cage

The True Spirit of Sisters

Sisters can be sweet sometimes and not so sweet other times. They can be silly and fun or serious and demanding. They can be happy and easygoing or a bit grumpy and hardheaded. But whatever words you use to describe sisters, you can never really capture their true spirit, because... A sister's true spirit is found in her sensitive and caring feelings that are there when you need them. That's just the way sisters are.

I hope the next time you stop and think of me, you'll remember how much I care about you and know that we'll always be close; we'll always have each other.

~ Dena DiJaconi

I've Been Blessed
with a Beautiful Sister!

Maybe someday I'll be able to find all the right words to tell you how much you mean to me. In the meantime, I just hope you know, deep within your heart, that having you as my sister is a gift I thank my lucky stars for.

You're such a precious part of my life. Our family ties and our deep, lasting friendship comprise a special love that always sees me through. If I hadn't been blessed with such a beautiful sister, I would have spent a lifetime... wishing for someone just like you.

~ Laurel Atherton

You Deserve
All the Best, Sister

Of all the people I know, you are the one who deserves all the happiness in the world. I don't know anyone with a stronger, more generous heart than yours. I can feel its love reaching out every time I think of you.

If you have any doubts that you deserve all the best, please know that I see these wonderful qualities in you...

You are such an inspiration. You know what is right and you don't let anything or anyone sway you.

You embrace everyone you meet with immediate kindness. The sparkle in your eye puts everyone at ease.

You have a way of understanding other's troubles and finding a way to relate to them, and that is so comforting. I am always amazed at how much better I feel after talking to you for just a few minutes.

You are so talented. There are so many things that you excel at, and you encourage others by your example.

You are dedicated to whatever you start. You follow through with your dreams and almost always reach your highest goals.

But most of all, Sister, we share a bond that has strengthened us through both great times and difficult times. I want you to know how special every part of you is to me. I don't know what I'd do without you. So, I just wanted to take a moment to thank you for your love and to wish you the best in everything you do.

~ Jane Andrews

Sister, May You Always Have...

Cheer to greet you each morning, so that each new day will help you believe that you are one step closer to your dreams.

Peace in your inner being, so that you can breathe easy and enjoy every moment of your life.

Faith to encourage and inspire you; to comfort you and heal your hurts; to commune with and be one with; to help you get in touch with your true self.

Laughter to bring you happiness and fun and keep your joy alive; to remind you that life is too short to spend it crying.

Beauty to fill your eyes with the simple gifts that nature brings.

Confidence to do all the things that your true self desires; to conquer your fears and be free to reach your goals.

Friendships that are lasting and true with people who respect your values and are full of sharing and caring.

Memories that are warm and comforting, that you can reflect on and smile about; memories of our times together ~ loving memories that last a long while.

~ Jacqueline Schiff

You Are a Very Special Sister

I want you to know how amazing you are.
I want you to know how much you're
treasured and celebrated and quietly thanked.

I want you to feel really good...
   about who you are.
About all the great things you do!
I want you to appreciate your uniqueness.
Acknowledge your talents and abilities.
Realize what a beautiful soul you have.
Understand the wonder within.

You make so much sun shine through, and you inspire so much joy in the lives of everyone who is lucky enough to know you.

You are a very special person, giving so many people a reason to smile. You deserve to receive the best in return, and one of my heart's favorite hopes is that the happiness you give away will come back to warm you each and every day of your life.

~ Sydney Nealson

I'm Glad You're
My Sister

Have I ever told you
how glad I am
that you're my sister?
I'm telling you now
because I want you to know
how very important you are to me
and just how much love
there is for you
deep within my heart.

Too often, the beautiful things in life
are taken for granted,
and I realize that you
are one of the most beautiful
aspects of mine.
That's why it's so important
for me to tell you now
that you are special to me.

You're more than just family;
you are a friend,
a confidante,
and a shoulder to lean on
in times of need.
You're the person I always
want to share everything with ~
each dream, each goal I attain,
each sorrow, each joy.
If I have never told you before
how glad I am
that you're my sister,
I'm telling you now.
I want you to know
that you mean the world to me,
and I love you
with all my heart.

~ Deanne Laura Gilbert

Sisters Carry Each Other in Their Hearts Forever and Always

Whether they live near each other or far apart, sisters walk through life together. They're there for each other no matter what... sharing everything.

Sisters are connected at the heart and in their blood, and their loyalty to one another is permanent. No one can ever break that bond. They don't give up on each other easily. They have the utmost sensitivity and compassion for one another because they were born into the same family.

Sisters aren't afraid to break rules for each other. They defend each other; they take chances for each other. They've cried together and laughed together. They know each other's secrets. They forgive each other when they make mistakes, and they can almost read each other's minds.

Sisters teach each other lessons as they stand by each other in life, and they are there for each other through everything that matters.

No one can ever take the place of a sister. Thank you for being my sister. I carry you in my heart forever and always.

~ Donna Fargo

ACKNOWLEDGMENTS

The following is a partial list of authors whom the publisher especially wishes to thank for permission to reprint their works.

Shannon M. Lester for "Sister, You Are a Gift to Me." Copyright © 2002 by Shannon M. Lester. All rights reserved.

Jacqueline Schiff for "The Nine Secrets of Our Sisterhood." Copyright © 2002 by Jacqueline Schiff. All rights reserved.

Linda E. Knight for "A Sister's Love Is Something to Cherish." Copyright © 2002 by Linda E. Knight. All rights reserved.

PrimaDonna Entertainment Corp. for "Sisters Carry Each Other in Their Hearts Forever and Always" by Donna Fargo. Copyright © 2001 by PrimaDonna Entertainment Corp. All rights reserved.

A careful effort has been made to trace the ownership of poems used in this anthology in order to obtain permission to reprint copyrighted materials and give proper credit to the copyright owners. If any error or omission has occurred, it is completely inadvertent, and we would like to make corrections in future editions provided that written notification is made to the publisher:

SPS STUDIOS, INC., P.O. Box 4549, Boulder, Colorado 80306.